A Little Laughter

Compiled by Katherine Love

A Pocketful of Rhymes

A Little Laughter

A Little Laughter

Compiled by Katherine *Isabel* Love

Illustrated by Walter H. Lorraine

THOMAS Y. CROWELL COMPANY
New York

ACKNOWLEDGMENTS

*For the privilege of reprinting the copyrighted verses in this
book we extend grateful acknowledgment and thanks to the
following authors, publishers, literary agents and executors, and
estates:*

GEORGE ALLEN & UNWIN LTD. for Canadian permission for
"There Is an Inn, a Merry Old Inn" and "Troll Sat Alone on
His Seat of Stone" from *The Fellowship of the Ring* by J. R. R.
Tolkien, published by George Allen & Unwin Ltd.

MISS LOUISE ANDREWS for "I Wish that My Room Had a Floor"
from *Burgess Nonsense Book* by Gelett Burgess, published by
Frederick A. Stokes Company.

BEATRICE CURTIS BROWN for "Jonathan Bing" from *Jonathan
Bing and Other Verses* by Beatrice Curtis Brown, copyright
1936 by Beatrice Curtis Brown.

FABER AND FABER LIMITED for Canadian permission for "The
Song of the Jellicles" from *Old Possum's Book of Practical Cats*
by T. S. Eliot.

HARCOURT, BRACE AND COMPANY, INC., for "The Song of the
Jellicles" from *Old Possum's Book of Practical Cats,* copyright
1939 by T. S. Eliot, reprinted by permission of Harcourt, Brace
and Company, Inc.; and for "Circles" and "Mr. Pyme" from
The Little Hill, copyright 1949 by Harry Behn, reprinted by
permission of Harcourt, Brace and Company, Inc.

HARPER & BROTHERS for "A Dappled Duck" and "The Spangled
Pandemonium" from *Beyond the Pawpaw Trees* by Palmer
Brown, copyright 1954 by Palmer Brown; and for "Lucinda
Prattle" from *The Silver Nutmeg* by Palmer Brown, copyright
1956 by Palmer Brown.

CONTENTS

A Little Laughter

Three Little Puffins

Three little puffins
    Were partial to muffins,
As partial as partial can be.
    They wouldn't eat nuffin
    But hot buttered muffin
For breakfast and dinner and tea.
    Pantin' and puffin'
    And chewin' and chuffin'
They just went on stuffin', dear me!
    Till the three little puffins
    Were chockful of muffins
And puffy as puffy can be,
                All three
Were puffy as puffy can be.

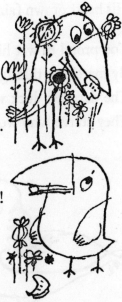

ELEANOR FARJEON

1

A Dappled Duck

A dappled duck with silver feet
Stood crying by a muddy street.
"I will not," wept the dappled duck,
"Soil silver feet with marshy muck."

From all the news that I can get,
That dappled duck is standing yet,
His feathers wet with dappled tears,
His heart grown faint with duckish fears.

Too proud to wet his silver feet
By marching through a muddy street,
The dappled duck will learn too late:
They starve who won't accept their fate.

PALMER BROWN

2

The Mice of Spain

The mice of Spain
Have little rain;
They sup on olive oil.

The mice of France
Drink wine and dance;
They have small use for toil.

The Chinese mice
All live on rice;
Their eyes are set aslant.

Mice, Hindu-born,
Eat sacred corn
And ride the elephant.

But as for us
We'll make no fuss
If we have bread and cheese.

All night we'll sing
In a scampering ring
And frolic as we please!

ELIZABETH COATSWORTH

Drinking Vessels

Barnaby Bloggin
Drank out of a noggin,
And Willoughby Wiggin,
Drank out of a piggin.
Gregory Graigh
Made use of a quaigh,
But I am much humbler,
I drink from a tumbler.

LAURA E. RICHARDS

The Merry Pieman's Song

"You are the cake of my endeavour, and my jelly-roll
    forever;
My tapioca-tartlet, my lemon-custard pie;
You're my candied fruit and spices, my juicy citron
    slices;
You're the darling, sugar-sprinkled apple-dumpling
    of my eye!"

JOHN BENNETT

If All The World Was Apple Pie

If all the world was apple pie,
    And all the sea was ink,
And all the trees were bread and cheese,
    What should we have for drink?

Bobbily Boo and Wollypotump

Bobbily Boo, the king so free,
He used to drink the Mango tea.
Mango tea and coffee, too,
He drank them both till his nose turned blue.

Wollypotump, the queen so high,
She used to eat the Gumbo pie.
Gumbo pie and Gumbo cake,
She ate them both till her teeth did break.

Bobbily Boo and Wollypotump,
Each called the other a greedy frump.
And when these terrible words were said,
They sat and cried till they both were dead.

LAURA E. RICHARDS

There Once Was a Man of Calcutta

There once was a man of Calcutta
Who spoke with a terrible stutter.
　At breakfast he said,
　"Give me b-b-b-bread,
And b-b-b-b-b-b-butter."

There Was an Old Man of Tarentum

There was an old man of Tarentum,
Who gnashed his false teeth till he bent 'em.
  When they asked him the cost
  Of what he had lost,
He replied, "I can't say, for I rent 'em."

An Epicure, Dining at Crewe

An epicure, dining at Crewe,
Found quite a large mouse in his stew.
  Said the waiter, "Don't shout,
  And wave it about,
Or the rest will be wanting one, too!"

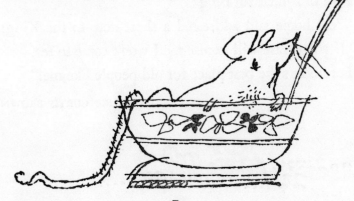

Jonathan Bing

Poor old Jonathan Bing
Went out in his carriage to visit the King,
But everyone pointed and said, "Look at that!
Jonathan Bing has forgotten his hat!"
(He'd forgotten his hat!)
Poor old Jonathan Bing
Went home and put on a new hat for the King,
But up by the palace a soldier said, "Hi!
You can't see the King; you've forgotten your tie!"
(He'd forgotten his tie!)
Poor old Jonathan Bing,
He put on a beautiful tie for the King,
But when he arrived an Archbishop said, "Ho!
You can't come to court in pyjamas, you know!"
Poor old Jonathan Bing
Went home and addressed a short note to the King:
"If you please will excuse me I won't come to tea,
For home's the best place for old people like me!"

BEATRICE CURTIS BROWN

8

Troll Sat Alone on His Seat of Stone

Troll sat alone on his seat of stone,
And munched and mumbled a bare old bone;
   For many a year he had gnawed it near,
     For meat was hard to come by.
       Done by! Gum by!
  In a cave in the hills he dwelt alone,
    And meat was hard to come by.

Up came Tom with his big boots on.
Said he to Troll: "Pray, what is yon?
   For it looks like the shin o' my nuncle Tim,
    As should be a-lyin' in graveyard.
      Caveyard! Paveyard!
  This many a year has Tim been gone,
    And I thought he were lyin' in graveyard."

"My lad," said Troll, "this bone I stole.
But what be bones that lie in a hole?
    Thy nuncle was dead as a lump o' lead,
        Afore I found his shinbone.
            Tinbone! Thinbone!
    He can spare a share for a poor old troll.
        For he don't need his shinbone."

Said Tom: "I don't see why the likes o' thee
Without axin' leave should go makin' free
    With the shank or the shin o' my father's kin;
        So hand the old bone over!
            Rover! Trover!
    Though dead he be, it belongs to he;
        So hand the old bone over!"

"For a couple o' pins," says Troll, and grins,
"I'll eat thee too, and gnaw thy shins.
    A bit o' fresh meat will go down sweet!
        I'll try my teeth on thee now.
            Hee now! See now!
    I'm tired o' gnawing old bones and skins;
        I've a mind to dine on thee now."

But just as he thought his dinner was caught,
He found his hands had hold of naught.
  Before he could mind, Tom slipped behind
    And gave him the boot to larn him.
        Warn him! Darn him!
  A bump o' the boot on the seat, Tom thought,
    Would be the way to larn him.

But harder than stone is the flesh and bone
Of a troll that sits in the hills alone.
  As well set your boot to the mountain's root:
    For the seat of a troll don't feel it.
        Peel it! Heal it!
  Old Troll laughed, when he heard Tom groan.
    And he knew his toes could feel it.

Tom's leg is game, since home he came,
And his bootless foot is lasting lame;
  But Troll don't care, and he's still there
    With the bone he boned from its owner.
        Doner! Boner!
  Troll's old seat is still the same,
    And the bone he boned from its owner!

J. R. R. TOLKIEN

1 1

The World Has Held Great Heroes

The world has held great Heroes,
  As history-books have showed;
But never a name to go down to fame
  Compared with that of Toad!

The clever men at Oxford
  Know all that there is to be knowed.
But they none of them know one half as much
  As intelligent Mr. Toad!

The animals sat in the Ark and cried,
  Their tears in torrents flowed.
Who was it said, "There's land ahead"?
  Encouraging Mr. Toad!

The Army all saluted
  As they marched along the road.
Was it the King? Or Kitchener?
  No. It was Mr. Toad!

The Queen and her Ladies-in-waiting
  Sat at the window and sewed.
She cried, "Look! who's that *handsome* man?"
  They answered, "Mr. Toad."

KENNETH GRAHAME

The Jumblies

They went to sea in a Sieve, they did,
   In a Sieve they went to sea:
In spite of all their friends could say,
On a winter's morn, on a stormy day,
   In a Sieve they went to sea!
And when the Sieve turned round and round,
And every one cried, "You'll all be drowned!"
They called aloud, "Our Sieve ain't big,
But we don't care a button, we don't care a fig!
   In a Sieve we'll go to sea!"
     Far and few, far and few,
       Are the lands where the Jumblies live;
       Their heads are green, and their hands are blue,
        And they went to sea in a Sieve.

They sailed away in a Sieve, they did,
　　In a Sieve they sailed so fast,
With only a beautiful pea-green veil
Tied with a ribbon, by way of a sail,
　　To a small tobacco-pipe mast;
And every one said, who saw them go,
"O won't they be soon upset, you know!
For the sky is dark, and the voyage is long,
And happen what may, it's extremely wrong
　　In a Sieve to sail so fast!"
　　　　Far and few, far and few,
　　　　　　Are the lands where the Jumblies live;
　　　　　Their heads are green, and their hands are blue,
　　　　　And they went to sea in a Sieve.

The water it soon came in, it did,
　　The water it soon came in;
So to keep them dry, they wrapped their feet
In a pinky paper all folded neat,
　　And they fastened it down with a pin.
And they passed the night in a crockery-jar,
And each of them said, "How wise we are!
Though the sky be dark, and the voyage be long,
Yet we never can think we were rash or wrong,

While round in our Sieve we spin!"
  Far and few, far and few,
    Are the lands where the Jumblies live;
    Their heads are green, and their hands are blue,
      And they went to sea in a Sieve.

And all night long they sailed away;
  And when the sun went down,
They whistled and warbled a moony song
To the echoing sound of a coppery gong,
  In the shade of the mountains brown.
"O Timballo! How happy we are,
When we live in a Sieve and a crockery-jar,
And all night long in the moonlight pale,
We sail away with a pea-green sail,
  In the shade of the mountains brown!"
    Far and few, far and few,
      Are the lands where the Jumblies live;
      Their heads are green, and their hands are blue,
        And they went to sea in a Sieve.

They sailed to the Western sea, they did,
  To a land all covered with trees,
And they bought an Owl, and a useful Cart,
And a pound of Rice, and a Cranberry Tart,
  And a hive of silvery Bees.
And they bought a Pig, and some green Jack-daws,
And a lovely Monkey with lollipop paws,
And forty bottles of Ring-Bo-Ree,
  And no end of Stilton Cheese.
    Far and few, far and few,
      Are the lands where the Jumblies live;
    Their heads are green, and their hands are blue,
      And they went to sea in a Sieve.

And in twenty years they all came back,
    In twenty years or more,
And every one said, "How tall they've grown!
For they've been to the Lakes, and the Torrible Zone,
    And the hills of the Chankly Bore."
And they drank their health, and gave them a feast
Of dumplings made of beautiful yeast;
And every one said, "If we only live,
We too will go to sea in a Sieve—
    To the hills of the Chankly Bore!"
        Far and few, far and few,
            Are the lands where the Jumblies live;
        Their heads are green, and their hands are blue,
            And they went to sea in a Sieve.

EDWARD LEAR

The Grandiloquent Goat

A very grandiloquent Goat
Sat down to a gay table d'hote;
   He ate all the corks,
   The knives and the forks,
Remarking: "On these things I dote."

Then, before his repast he began,
While pausing the menu to scan,
   He said: "Corn, if you please,
   And tomatoes and pease,
I'd like to have served in the can."

CAROLYN WELLS

1 8

The Guinea-Pig

There was a little guinea-pig,
Who, being little, was not big;
He always walked upon his feet,
And never fasted when he eat.

When from a place he ran away,
He never at that place did stay;
And while he ran, as I am told,
He ne'er stood still for young or old.

He often squeaked and sometimes vi'lent,
And when he squeaked he ne'er was silent;
Though ne'er instructed by a cat,
He knew a mouse was not a rat.

One day, as I am certified,
He took a whim and fairly died;
And as I'm told by men of sense,
He never has been living since.

19

The Frog

Be kind and tender to the Frog,
  And do not call him names,
As "Slimy skin," or "Polly-wog,"
  Or likewise "Ugly James,"
Or "Gap-a-grin," or "Toad-gone-wrong,"
  Or "Bill Bandy-knees":
The Frog is justly sensitive
  To epithets like these.

No animal will more repay
  A treatment kind and fair,
At least, so lonely people say
Who keep a frog (and, by the way,
  They are extremely rare).

HILAIRE BELLOC

20

The Lama

The one-l lama,
He's a priest.
The two-l llama,
He's a beast.
And I will bet
A silk pyjama
There isn't any
Three-l lllama.

OGDEN NASH

The Grasshopper

Down
a
deep
well
a
grasshopper
fell.

By kicking about
He thought to get out.

      He might have known better,
      For that got him wetter.
To kick round and round
Is the way to get drowned,
      And drowning is what
      I should tell you he got.

          But
          the
          well
          had
          a
          rope
          that
          dangled
          some
          hope.

And sure as molasses
On one of his passes
      He found the rope handy
      And up he went, *and he*

it
up
and
it
up
and
it
up
and
it
up
went

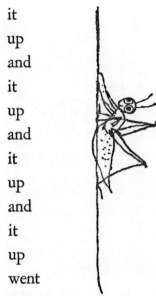

And hopped away proper
As any grasshopper.

DAVID MC CORD

Eletelephony

Once there was an elephant,
Who tried to use the telephant—
No! no! I mean an elephone
Who tried to use the telephone—
(Dear me! I am not certain quite
That even now I've got it right.)

Howe'er it was, he got his trunk
Entangled in the telephunk;
The more he tried to get it free,
The louder buzzed the telephee—
(I fear I'd better drop the song
Of elephop and telephong!)

LAURA E. RICHARDS

24

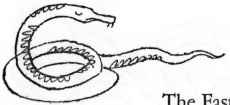

The Fastidious Serpent

There was a snake that dwelt in Skye,
    Over the misty sea, oh;
He lived upon nothing but gooseberry-pie
    For breakfast, dinner, and tea, oh.

Now gooseberry-pie—as is very well known—
    Over the misty sea, oh,
Is not to be found under every stone,
    Nor yet upon every tree, oh.

And being so ill to please with his meat,
    Over the misty sea, oh,
The snake had sometimes nothing to eat,
    And an angry snake was he, oh.

Then he'd flick his tongue and his head he'd shake,
    Over the misty sea, oh,
Crying, "Gooseberry-pie! For goodness' sake,
    Some gooseberry-pie for me, oh!"

And if gooseberry-pie was not to be had,
   Over the misty sea, oh,
He'd twine and twist like an eel gone mad,
   Or a worm just stung by a bee, oh.

But though he might shout and wriggle about,
   Over the misty sea, oh,
The snake had often to go without
   His breakfast, dinner, and tea, oh.

HENRY JOHNSTONE

Sage Counsel

The lion is the beast to fight:
  He leaps along the plain,
And if you run with all your might,
  He runs with all his mane.
    I'm glad I'm not a Hottentot,
    But if I were, with outward cal-lum
    I'd either faint upon the spot
    Or hie me up a leafy pal-lum.

The Chamois is the beast to hunt:
  He's fleeter than the wind,
And when the Chamois is in front
  The hunter is behind.

The Tyrolese make famous cheese
And hunt the Chamois o'er the chaz-zums;
I'd choose the former, if you please,
For precipices give me spaz-zums.

The Polar Bear will make a rug
  Almost as white as snow:
But if he gets you in his hug,
  He rarely lets you go.
    And polar ice looks very nice,
    With all the colors of a prissum:
    But, if you'll follow my advice,
    Stay home and learn your catechissum.

ARTHUR QUILLER-COUCH

There Was a Young Lady of Niger

There was a young lady of Niger
Who smiled as she rode on a tiger;
    They returned from the ride
    With the lady inside,
And the smile on the face of the tiger.

COSMO MONKHOUSE

The Panther

The panther is like a leopard,
Except it hasn't been peppered.
Should you behold a panther crouch,
Prepare to say Ouch.
Better yet, if called by a panther,
Don't anther.

OGDEN NASH

Higglety, Pigglety, Pop!

Higglety, pigglety, pop!
The dog has eaten the mop;
   The pig's in a hurry,
   The cat's in a flurry,
Higglety, pigglety, pop!

SAMUEL GOODRICH

Advice to Young Naturalists

Did you ever attempt to shampoo
    A Gnu?
I do not advise you to try.
He is apt to retort
With a sniff and a snort,
And you may find his horn in your eye.

Did you ever endeavor to scale
    A Whale?
Believe me, 'twould be a mistake.
He would offer rebuke
With a flip of his fluke,
And your bones would most probably break.

P.S. *Besides, he has no scales!*

LAURA E. RICHARDS

31

The Kilkenny Cats

There once were two cats of Kilkenny.
Each thought there was one cat too many;
So they fought and they fit,
And they scratched and they bit,
  Till, excepting their nails,
  And the tips of their tails,
Instead of two cats, there weren't any.

The Camel

The camel has a single hump;
The dromedary, two;
Or else the other way around.
I'm never sure. Are you?

OGDEN NASH

The Common Cormorant

The common cormorant or shag
Lays eggs inside a paper bag
The reason you will see no doubt
It is to keep the lightning out.
But what these unobservant birds
Have never noticed is that herds
Of wandering bears may come with buns
And steal the bags to hold the crumbs.

33

How Doth the Little Crocodile

How doth the little crocodile
   Improve his shining tail,
And pour the waters of the Nile
   On every golden scale!

How cheerfully he seems to grin,
   How neatly spreads his claws,
And welcomes little fishes in,
   With gently smiling jaws!

LEWIS CARROLL

A Centipede Was Happy Quite

A centipede was happy quite,
Until a frog in fun
Said, "Pray, which leg comes after which?"
This raised her mind to such a pitch
She lay distracted in the ditch
Considering how to run.

MRS. EDWARD CRASTER

The Elephant

When people call this beast to mind,
    They marvel more and more
At such a little tail behind,
    So LARGE a trunk before.

HILAIRE BELLOC

The Pelican Chorus

King and Queen of the Pelicans we;
No other Birds so grand we see!
None but we have feet like fins!
With lovely leathery throats and chins!
  Ploffskin, Pluffskin, Pelican jee!
  We think no Birds so happy as we!
  Plumpskin, Ploshkin, Pelican jill!
  We think so then, and we thought so still!

We live on the Nile. The Nile we love.
By night we sleep on the cliffs above;
By day we fish, and at eve we stand
On long bare islands of yellow sand.
And when the sun sinks slowly down
And the great rock walls grow dark and brown,
Where the purple river rolls fast and dim
And the Ivory Ibis starlike skim,
Wing to wing we dance around,—
Stamping our feet with a flumpy sound,—
Opening our mouths as Pelicans ought,
And this is the song we nightly snort;—

Ploffskin, Pluffskin, Pelican jee,
We think no Birds so happy as we!
Plumpskin, Ploshkin, Pelican jill,
We think so then, and we thought so still!

Last year came out our Daughter, Dell;
And all the Birds received her well.
To do her honour, a feast we made
For every bird that can swim or wade.
Herons and Gulls, and Cormorants black,
Cranes, and Flamingoes with scarlet back.
Plovers and Storks, and Geese in clouds,
Swans and Dilberry Ducks in crowds.

Thousands of Birds in wondrous flight!
They ate and drank and danced all night,
And echoing back from the rocks you heard
Multitude-echoes from Bird and Bird,—

Ploffskin, Pluffskin, Pelican jee,
We think no Birds so happy as we!
Plumpskin, Ploshkin, Pelican jill,
We think so then, and we thought so still!

Yes, they came; and among the rest,
The King of the Cranes all grandly dressed.
Such a lovely tail! Its feathers float
Between the ends of his blue dress-coat;
With pea-green trowsers all so neat,
And a delicate frill to hide his feet,—
(For though no one speaks of it, every one knows,
He has got no webs between his toes!)
As soon as he saw our Daughter Dell,
In violent love that Crane King fell,—

On seeing her waddling form so fair,
With a wreath of shrimps in her short white hair.
And before the end of the next long day,
Our Dell had given her heart away;
For the King of the Cranes had won that heart,
With a Crocodile's egg and a large fish-tart.
She vowed to marry the King of the Cranes,
Leaving the Nile for stranger plains;
And away they flew in a gathering crowd
Of endless birds in a lengthening cloud.

Ploffskin, Pluffskin, Pelican jee,
We think no Birds so happy as we!
Plumpskin, Ploshkin, Pelican jill,
We think so then, and we thought so still!

And far away in the twilight sky,
We heard them singing a lessening cry,—
Farther and farther till out of sight,
And we stood alone in the silent night!
Often since, in the nights of June,
We sit on the sand and watch the moon;—
She has gone to the great Gromboolian plain,
And we probably never shall meet again!
Oft, in the long still nights of June,
We sit on the rocks and watch the moon;—
She dwells by the streams of the Chankly Bore,
And we probably never shall see her more.
Ploffskin, Pluffskin, Pelican jee,
We think no Birds so happy as we!
Plumpskin, Ploshkin, Pelican jill,
We think so then, and we thought so still!

EDWARD LEAR

Three Young Rats

Three young rats with black felt hats,
Three young ducks with white straw flats,
Three young dogs with curling tails,
Three young cats with demi-veils,
Went out to walk with two young pigs
In satin vests and sorrel wigs;
But suddenly it chanced to rain
And so they all went home again.

The Ostrich Is a Silly Bird

The ostrich is a silly bird,
　　With scarcely any mind.
He often runs so very fast,
　　He leaves himself behind.

And when he gets there, has to stand
　　And hang about till night,
Without a blessed thing to do
　　Until he comes in sight.

MARY E. WILKINS FREEMAN

Ode to the Pig: His Tail

My tail is not impressive
   But it's elegant and neat.
In length it's not excessive—
   I can't curl it round my feet—
But it's awfully expressive,
And its weight is not excessive,
   And I *don't* think it's conceit,
   Or foolishly possessive
If I state with some aggressive-
   ness that it's the final master touch
That makes a pig complete.

WALTER R. BROOKS

The Prince

Sweet Peridarchus was a Prince,
The Prince he was of—Mouses;
He roved and roamed the haunts of Men,
And ranged about their houses.

He gnawed his way along a street,
Through holes in every wainscot,
Fandangoed in the attics and
From basement on to basement.

His eyes like bits of rubies shone;
His coat, as sleek as satin—
With teeth as sharp as needle-points—
He kept to keep him fat in.

His squeak so sharp in the small hours rang
That every waker wondered;
He trimmed his whiskers stiff as wire,
Had sweethearts by the hundred.

He'd gut a Cheshire cheese with ease,
Plum cake devoured in slices,
Lard, haggis, suet, sausages,
And everything that nice is.

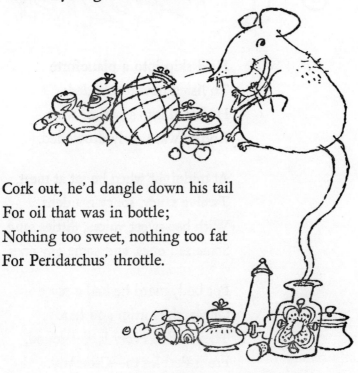

Cork out, he'd dangle down his tail
For oil that was in bottle;
Nothing too sweet, nothing too fat
For Peridarchus' throttle.

He'd dance upon a chimney-pot,
The merry stars a-twinkling;
Or, scampering up a chandelier,
Set all the lustres tinkling.

He'd skip into a pianoforte
To listen how it sounded;
He bored into a butt of wine,
And so was nearly drownded.

At midnight when he sat at meat,
Twelve saucy, soncy maidens,
With bee-sweet voices, ditties sang,
Some sad ones, and some gay ones.

For bodyguard he had a score
Of warriors grim and hardy;
They raided every larder round,
From Peebles to—Cromàrty.

Grimalkin—deep in dreams she lay,
Comes he, with these gay friskers,
Steals up and gnaws away her claws,
And plucks out all her whiskers.

He scaled a bell-rope where there snored
The Bailiff and his Lady;
Danced on his nose, nibbled her toes,
And kissed the squalling Baby.

A merry life was his, I trow,
Despite it was a short one;
One night he met a mort of rats—
He bared his teeth, and fought one:

A bully ruffian, thrice his size;
But when the conflict ended,
He sighed, "Alack, my back is broke,
And that can ne'er be mended."

They laid him lifeless on a bier,
They lapped him up in ermine;
They lit a candle, inches thick,
His Uncle preached the sermon.

"O Mouseland, mourn for him that's gone,
Our noble Peridarchus!
In valiant fight but yesternight,
And now, alas, a carcass!

"A Hero, Mouse or Man, is one
Who never wails or winces;
Friends, shed a tear for him that's here,
The Princeliest of Princes!"

WALTER DE LA MARE

A Flea and a Fly in a Flue

A flea and a fly in a flue
Were imprisoned, so what could they do?
  Said the fly, "Let us flee,"
  Said the flea, "Let us fly,"
So they flew through a flaw in the flue.

A Tutor Who Tooted the Flute

A Tutor who tooted the flute
Tried to teach two young tooters to toot;
  Said the two to the Tutor,
  "Is it harder to toot, or
To tutor two tooters to toot?"

CAROLYN WELLS

49

The Song of the Jellicles

Jellicle Cats come out to-night,
Jellicle Cats come one come all:
The Jellicle Moon is shining bright—
Jellicles come to the Jellicle Ball.

Jellicle Cats are black and white,
Jellicle Cats are rather small;
Jellicle Cats are merry and bright,
And pleasant to hear when they caterwaul.
Jellicle Cats have cheerful faces,
Jellicle Cats have bright black eyes;
They like to practise their airs and graces
And wait for the Jellicle Moon to rise.

Jellicle Cats develop slowly,
Jellicle Cats are not too big;
Jellicle Cats are roly-poly,
They know how to dance a gavotte and a jig.
Until the Jellicle Moon appears
They make their toilette and take their repose:
Jellicles wash behind their ears,
Jellicles dry between their toes.

Jellicle Cats are white and black,
Jellicle Cats are of moderate size;
Jellicles jump like a jumping-jack,
Jellicle Cats have moonlit eyes.
They're quiet enough in the morning hours,
They're quiet enough in the afternoon,
Reserving their terpsichorean powers
To dance by the light of the Jellicle Moon.

Jellicle Cats are black and white,
Jellicle Cats (as I said) are small;
If it happens to be a stormy night
They will practise a caper or two in the hall.
If it happens the sun is shining bright
You would say they had nothing to do at all:
They are resting and saving themselves to be right
For the Jellicle Moon and the Jellicle Ball.

T. S. ELIOT

Theophilus Thistledown

Theophilus Thistledown, the successful thistle sifter,
In sifting a sieve of unsifted thistles,
Thrust three thousand thistles
Through the thick of his thumb.
If, then, Theophilus Thistledown, the successful thistle
    sifter,
In sifting a sieve full of unsifted thistles,
Thrust three thousand thistles
Through the thick of his thumb,
See that thou, in sifting a sieve of unsifted thistles,
Do not get the unsifted thistles stuck in thy tongue.

Circles

The things to draw with compasses
Are suns and moons and circleses
And rows of humptydumpasses
Or anything in circuses
Like hippopotamusseses
And hoops and camels' humpasses
And wheels on clownses busseses
And fat old elephumpasses.

HARRY BEHN

A Sleeper from the Amazon

A sleeper from the Amazon
Put nighties of his gra'mazon—
    The reason, that
    He was too fat
To get his own pajamazon.

The Bees' Song

Thouzandz of thornz there be
On the Rozez where gozez
The Zebra of Zee:
Sleek, striped, and hairy,
The steed of the Fairy
Princess of Zee.

Heavy with blozzomz be
The Rozez that growzez
In the thickets of Zee,
Where grazez the Zebra,
Marked Abracadeeebra
Of the Princess of Zee.

And he nozez the poziez
Of the Rozez that growzez
So luvez'm and free,
With an eye, dark and wary,
In search of a Fairy,

Whose Rozez he knowzez
Were not honeyed for he,
But to breathe a sweet incense
To solace the Princess
Of far-away Zee.

WALTER DE LA MARE

There Was an Old Man of Blackheath

There was an old man of Blackheath,
Who sat on his set of false teeth.
  Said he, with a start,
  "Oh Lord, bless my heart!
I've bitten myself underneath!"

Mr. Finney's Turnip

Mr. Finney had a turnip
  And it grew behind the barn;
And it grew and it grew,
  And that turnip did no harm.

There it grew and it grew
  Till it could grow no longer;
Then his daughter Lizzie picked it
  And put it in the cellar.

There it lay and it lay
  Till it began to rot;
And his daughter Susie took it
  And put it in the pot.

And they boiled it and boiled it
  As long as they were able;
And then his daughters took it
  And put it on the table.

Mr. Finney and his wife
  They sat them down to sup;
And they ate and they ate
  And they ate that turnip up.

Mumps

I had a feeling in my neck,
  And on the sides were two big bumps;
I couldn't swallow anything
  At all because I had the mumps.

And Mother tied it with a piece,
  And then she tied up Will and John,
And no one else but Dick was left
  That didn't have a mump rag on.

He teased at us and laughed at us,
  And said, whenever he went by,

"It's vinegar and lemon-drops
   And pickles!" just to make us cry.

But Tuesday Dick was very sad
   And cried because his neck was sore,
And not a one said sour things
   To anybody any more.

ELIZABETH MADOX ROBERTS

If All the Seas Were One Sea

If all the seas were one sea,
What a *great* sea that would be!
And if all the trees were one tree,
What a *great* tree that would be!
And if all the axes were one axe,
What a *great* axe that would be!
And if all the men were one man,
What a *great* man he would be!
And if the *great* man took the *great* axe,
And cut down the *great* tree,
And let it fall into the *great* sea,
What a splish splash *that* would be!

59

The Great Panjandrum Himself

So she went into the garden to cut a
cabbage-leaf
to make an apple-pie;
and at the same time a great she-bear,
coming down the street, pops its head
into the shop.
What! No soap?
So he died,
and she very imprudently married the
Barber:
and there were present
the Picninnies, and the Joblillies,
and the Garyulies,
and the Great Panjandrum himself, with
the little round button at top;
and they all fell to playing the game of
catch-as-catch-can,
till the gunpowder ran out at the heels
of their boots.

SAMUEL FOOTE

Little John Bottlejohn

Little John Bottlejohn lived on the hill,
   And a blithe little man was he.
And he won the heart of a pretty mermaid
   Who lived in the deep blue sea.
And every evening she used to sit

And sing on the rocks by the sea,
"Oh! little John Bottlejohn, pretty John Bottlejohn,
   Won't you come out to me?"

Little John Bottlejohn heard her song,
   And he opened his little door.
And he hopped and he skipped, and he skipped and he
   hopped,
   Until he came down to the shore.
And there on the rocks sat the little mermaid,
   And still she was singing so free,
"Oh! little John Bottlejohn, pretty John Bottlejohn,
   Won't you come out to me?"

Little John Bottlejohn made a bow,
   And the mermaid, she made one too;
And she said, "Oh! I never saw any one half
   So perfectly sweet as you!
In my lovely home 'neath the ocean foam,
   How happy we both might be!
"Oh! little John Bottlejohn, pretty John Bottlejohn,
   Won't you come down with me?"

Little John Bottlejohn said, "Oh yes!
   I'll willingly go with you.
And I never shall quail at the sight of your tail,
   For perhaps I may grow one too."
So he took her hand, and he left the land,
   And plunged in the foaming main.
And little John Bottlejohn, pretty John Bottlejohn,
   Never was seen again.

LAURA E. RICHARDS

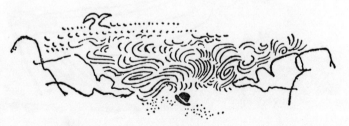

63

As I Was Going to Derby

As I was going to Derby,
  Upon a market day,
I met the finest ram, sir,
  That ever was fed on hay.

This ram was fat behind, sir,
  This ram was fat before,
This ram was ten yards high, sir,
  Indeed he was no more.

The wool upon his back, sir,
  Reached up into the sky,
The eagles built their nests there,
  For I heard the young ones cry.

The space between the horns, sir,
  Was as far as man could reach,
And there they built a pulpit,
  But no-one in it preached.

This ram had four legs to walk upon,
  This ram had four legs to stand,
And every leg he had, sir,
  Stood on an acre of land.

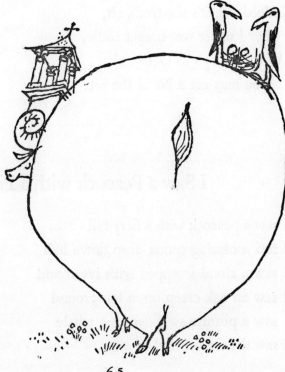

Now the man that fed the ram, sir,
  He fed him twice a day,
And each time that he fed him, sir,
  He ate a rick of hay.

The man that killed this ram, sir,
  Was up to his knees in blood,
And the boy that held the pail, sir,
  Was carried away in the flood.

Indeed, sir, it's the truth, sir,
  For I never was taught to lie,
And if you go to Derby, sir,
  You may eat a bit of the pie.

I Saw a Peacock with a Fiery Tail

I saw a peacock with a fiery tail
I saw a blazing comet drop down hail
I saw a cloud wrapped with ivy round
I saw an oak creep upon the ground
I saw a pismire swallow up a whale
I saw the sea brimful of ale

I saw a Venice glass full fifteen feet deep
I saw a well full of men's tears that weep
I saw red eyes all of a flaming fire
I saw a house bigger than the moon and higher
I saw the sun at twelve o'clock at night
I saw the Man that saw this wondrous sight.

Calico Pie

Calico Pie,
  The little Birds fly
Down to the calico tree,
  Their wings were blue,
  And they sang "Tilly-loo!"
Till away they flew,—
    And they never came back to me!
    They never came back!
    They never came back!
  They never came back to me!

Calico Jam,
The little Fish swam,
Over the syllabub sea,
He took off his hat,
To the Sole and the Sprat,
And the Willeby-wat,—
But he never came back to me!
He never came back!
He never came back!
He never came back to me!

Calico Ban,
The little Mice ran,
To be ready in time for tea,
Flippity flup,
They drank it all up,
And danced in the cup,—
But they never came back to me!
They never came back!
They never came back!
They never came back to me!

Calico Drum,
   The Grasshoppers come,
The Butterfly, Beetle, and Bee,
   Over the ground,
   Around and round,
   With a hop and a bound,—
      But they never came back!
         They never came back!
         They never came back!
      They never came back to me!

EDWARD LEAR

The Dodo

The Dodo used to walk around,
   And take the sun and air.
The sun yet warms his native ground—
   The Dodo is not there!

The voice which used to squawk and squeak
   Is now for ever dumb—
Yet may you see his bones and beak
   All in the Mu-se-um.

HILAIRE BELLOC

The Spangled Pandemonium

The Spangled Pandemonium
Is missing from the zoo.
He bent the bars the barest bit,
And slithered glibly through.

He crawled across the moated wall,
He climbed the mango tree,
And when his keeper scrambled up,
He nipped him in the knee.

To all of you, a warning
Not to wander after dark,

Or if you must, make very sure
You stay out of the park.

For the Spangled Pandemonium
Is missing from the zoo,
And since he nipped his keeper,
He would just as soon nip you!

PALMER BROWN

The Horny-Goloch Is an Awesome Beast

The horny-goloch is an awesome beast,
Soople an scaly;
It has twa horns, an a hantle o feet,
An a forkie tailie.

The Pobble Who Has No Toes

The Pobble who has no toes
   Had once as many as we;
When they said, "Some day you may lose them all,"—
   He replied,—"Fish fiddle de-dee!"
And his Aunt Jobiska made him drink,
Lavender water tinged with pink,
For she said, "The World in general knows
There's nothing so good for a Pobble's toes!"

The Pobble who has no toes,
   Swam across the Bristol Channel;
But before he set out he wrapped his nose,
   In a piece of scarlet flannel.
For his Aunt Jobiska said, "No harm
Can come to his toes if his nose is warm;

And it's perfectly known that a Pobble's toes
Are safe,—provided he minds his nose."

The Pobble swam fast and well,
    And when boats and ships came near him,
He tinkledy-binkledy-winkled a bell
    So that all the world could hear him.

And all the Sailors and Admirals cried,
When they saw him nearing the further side,—
"He has gone to fish for his Aunt Jobiska's
Runcible Cat with crimson whiskers!"

But before he touched the shore,
    The shore of the Bristol Channel,
A sea-green Porpoise carried away

His wrapper of scarlet flannel.
And when he came to observe his feet,
Formerly garnished with toes so neat,
His face at once became forlorn
On perceiving that all his toes were gone!

And nobody ever knew,
  From that dark day to the present,
Whoso had taken the Pobble's toes,
  In a manner so far from pleasant.
Whether the shrimps or crawfish gray,
Or crafty Mermaids stole them away—
Nobody knew; and nobody knows
How the Pobble was robbed of his twice five toes!

The Pobble who has no toes
  Was placed in a friendly Bark,
And they rowed him back and carried him up
  To his Aunt Jobiska's Park.
And she made him a feast at his earnest wish,
Of eggs and buttercups fried with fish;—
And she said,—"It's a fact the whole world knows,
That Pobbles are happier without their toes."

EDWARD LEAR

I Never Saw a Purple Cow

I never saw a Purple Cow,
  I never hope to see one;
But I can tell you, anyhow,
  I'd rather see than be one!

GELETT BURGESS

In a Cottage in Fife

In a cottage in Fife
  Lived a man and his wife,
Who, believe me, were comical folk;
  For, to people's surprise,
  They both saw with their eyes,
And their tongues moved whenever they spoke.
  When quite fast asleep,
  I've been told that to keep
Their eyes open they could not contrive;
  They walked on their feet,
  And 'twas thought what they eat
Helped, with drinking, to keep them alive.

I Wish that My Room Had a Floor

I wish that my Room had a Floor;
I don't so much care for a Door,
    But this walking around
    Without touching the ground
Is getting to be quite a bore!

GELETT BURGESS

King Pippin

Little King Pippin
  He built a fine hall,
Pie-crust and pastry-crust
  That was the wall;
The windows were made
  Of black pudding and white,
And slated with pancakes,
  You ne'er saw the like.

The Vulture

The Vulture eats between his meals,
   And that's the reason why
He very, very rarely feels
   As well as you and I.

His eye is dull, his head is bald,
   His neck is growing thinner.
Oh! what a lesson for us all
   To only eat at dinner.

HILAIRE BELLOC

Lucinda Prattle

Lucinda Prattle, foolish froth!
   Was warned when she was young
To spare her breath to cool her broth.
   She scoffed—and wagged her tongue.

Her birthday cake, with candles lit,
   Stood twinkling on the table.

"Blow! Lucinda. Don't just sit!"
 She tried—and was not able!

The candles blazed, the frosting boiled,
 The plate grew hot to touch.
Lucinda wept. Her cake was spoiled,
 Because—she'd talked too much!

Her windy words, Lucinda learned,
 Were better kept in storage,
To save her cake from being burned,
 Or cool her soup and porridge.

PALMER BROWN

Jim

Who ran away from his Nurse, and was eaten by a Lion.

There was a Boy whose name was Jim;
His Friends were very good to him.
They gave him Tea, and Cakes, and Jam,
And slices of delicious Ham,
And Chocolate with pink inside,
And little Tricycles to ride,
And read him Stories through and through,
And even took him to the Zoo—
But there it was the dreadful Fate
Befell him, which I now relate.

You know—at least you *ought* to know,
For I have often told you so—
That Children never are allowed
To leave their Nurses in a Crowd;
Now this was Jim's especial Foible,
He ran away when he was able,
And on this inauspicious day
He slipped his hand and ran away!
He hadn't gone a yard when—Bang!
With open Jaws, a Lion sprang,
And hungrily began to eat
The Boy: beginning at his feet.

Now just imagine how it feels
When first your toes and then your heels,
And then by gradual degrees,
Your shins and ankles, calves and knees,
Are slowly eaten, bit by bit.
No wonder Jim detested it!
No wonder that he shouted "Hi!"
The Honest Keeper heard his cry,
Though very fat he almost ran
To help the little gentleman.
"Ponto!" he ordered as he came
(For Ponto was the Lion's name),
"Ponto!" he cried, with angry Frown.
"Let go, Sir! Down, Sir! Put it down!"
The Lion made a sudden Stop,
He let the Dainty Morsel drop,
And slunk reluctant to his Cage,
Snarling with Disappointed Rage
But when he bent him over Jim,
The Honest Keeper's Eyes were dim.
The Lion having reached his Head,
The Miserable Boy was dead!

When Nurse informed his Parents, they
Were more Concerned than I can say:—
His Mother, as She dried her eyes,
Said, "Well—it gives me no surprise,
He would not do as he was told!"
His Father, who was self-controlled,
Bade all the children round attend
To James' miserable end,
And always keep a-hold of Nurse
For fear of finding something worse.

HILAIRE BELLOC

Anna Elise, She Jumped with Surprise

Anna Elise, she jumped with surprise;
The surprise was so quick, it played her a trick;
The trick was so rare, she jumped in a chair;
The chair was so frail, she jumped in a pail;
The pail was so wet, she jumped in a net;
The net was so small, she jumped on the ball;
The ball was so round, she jumped on the ground;
And ever since then she's been turning around.

The Akond of Swat

Who, or why, or which, or *what*

                Is the Akond of SWAT?

Is he tall or short, or dark or fair?

Does he sit on a stool or a sofa or chair,

                or SQUAT,

                  The Akond of Swat?

Is he wise or foolish, young or old?

Does he drink his soup and his coffee cold,

                or HOT,

                  The Akond of Swat?

Does he sing or whistle, jabber or talk,

And when riding abroad does he gallop or walk,

                or TROT,

                  The Akond of Swat?

Does he wear a turban, a fez, or a hat?
Does he sleep on a mattress, a bed or a mat,

     or a COT,

      The Akond of Swat?

When he writes a copy in round-hand size,
Does he cross his T's and finish his I's

     with a DOT,

      The Akond of Swat?

Can he write a letter concisely clear
Without a speck or a smudge or smear

     or BLOT,

      The Akond of Swat?

Do his people like him extremely well?
Or do they, whenever they can, rebel,

     or PLOT,

      At the Akond of Swat?

If he catches them then, either old or young,
Does he have them chopped in pieces or hung,

     or *shot*,

      The Akond of Swat?

Do his people prig in the lanes or park?
Or even at times, when days are dark,

     GAROTTE?

      O the Akond of Swat!

Does he study the wants of his own dominion?
Or doesn't he care for public opinion

                           a JOT,
                              The Akond of Swat?

To amuse his mind do his people show him
Pictures, or any one's last new poem,

                           or WHAT,
                              For the Akond of Swat?

At night if he suddenly screams and wakes,
Do they bring him only a few small cakes,

                           or a LOT,
                              For the Akond of Swat?

Does he live on turnips, tea, or tripe?
Does he like his shawl to be marked with a stripe,

                           or a DOT,
                              The Akond of Swat?

Does he like to lie on his back in a boat
Like the lady who lived in that isle remote,

                           SHALLOTT,
                              The Akond of Swat?

Is he quiet, or always making a fuss?
Is his steward a Swiss or a Swede or a Russ,

                           or a SCOT,
                              The Akond of Swat?

Does he like to sit by the calm blue wave?
Or to sleep and snore in a dark green cave,

>   or a GROTT,
>   The Akond of Swat?

Does he drink small beer from a silver jug?
Or a bowl? or a glass? or a cup? or a mug?

>   or a POT,
>   The Akond of Swat?

Does he beat his wife with a gold-topped pipe,
When she lets the gooseberries grow too ripe,

>   or ROT,
>   The Akond of Swat?

Does he wear a white tie when he dines with friends,
And tie it neat in a bow with ends,

>   or a KNOT,
>   The Akond of Swat?

Does he like new cream, and hate mince-pies?
When he looks at the sun does he wink his eyes,

>   or NOT,
>   The Akond of Swat?

Does he teach his subjects to roast and bake?
Does he sail about on an inland lake,

>   in a YACHT,
>   The Akond of Swat?

Some one, or nobody, knows I wot
Who or which or why or what

                Is the Akond of Swat!

EDWARD LEAR

B

B's the Bus,
The bouncing Bus,
   That bears a shopper store-ward.
It's fun to sit
In back of it
   But seats are better forward.
Although it's big as buildings are
   And looks both bold and grand,
It has to stop obligingly
   If you but raise your hand.

PHYLLIS MC GINLEY

E is the Escalator
　　That gives an elegant ride.
You step on the stair
With an easy air
　　And up and up you glide.
It's nicer than scaling ladders
　　Or scrambling 'round a hill,
For you climb and climb
But all the time
　　You're really standing still.

PHYLLIS MC GINLEY

The Walloping Window-blind

A capital ship for an ocean trip
　　Was *The Walloping Window-blind;*
No gale that blew dismayed her crew
　　Or troubled the captain's mind.

The man at the wheel was taught to feel
　Contempt for the wildest blow,
And it often appeared, when the weather had cleared,
　That he'd been in his bunk below.

The boatswain's mate was very sedate,
　Yet fond of amusement, too;
And he played hop-scotch with the starboard watch
　While the captain tickled the crew.
And the gunner we had was apparently mad,
　For he sat on the after-rail,
And fired salutes with the captain's boots,
　In the teeth of the blooming gale.

The captain sat in a commodore's hat,
    And dined, in a royal way,
On toasted pigs and pickles and figs
    And gummery bread, each day.
But the cook was Dutch, and behaved as such;
    For the food that he gave the crew
Was a number of tons of hot-cross buns,
    Chopped up with sugar and glue.

And we all felt ill as mariners will,
    On a diet that's cheap and rude;
And we shivered and shook as we dipped the cook
    In a tub of his gluesome food.
Then nautical pride we laid aside,
    And we cast the vessel ashore
On the Gulliby Isles, where the Poohpooh smiles,
    And the Anagazanders roar.

Composed of sand was that favored land,
  And trimmed with cinnamon straws;
And pink and blue was the pleasing hue
  Of the Tickletoeteaser's claws.
And we sat on the edge of a sandy ledge
  And shot at the whistling bee;
And the Binnacle-bats wore water-proof hats
  As they danced in the sounding sea.

On rubagub bark, from dawn to dark,
  We fed, till we all had grown
Uncommonly shrunk,—when a Chinese junk
  Came by from the torriby zone.
She was stubby and square, but we didn't much care,
  And we cheerily put to sea;
And we left the crew of the junk to chew
  The bark of the rubagub tree.

CHARLES E. CARRYL

93

Mr. Pyme

Once upon a time
Old Mr. Pyme
Lived all alone
Under a stone.

When the rain fell
He rang a bell,
When the sun shined
He laughed and dined

And floated to town
On thistle down,
And what a nice time
Had Mr. Pyme!

HARRY BEHN

94

Edouard

A bugler named Dougal MacDougal
Found ingenious ways to be frugal.
He learned how to sneeze
In various keys,
Thus saving the price of a bugle.

OGDEN NASH

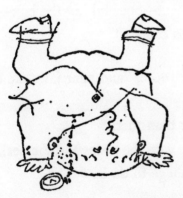

Father William

"You are old, Father William," the young man said,
 "And your hair has become very white;
And yet you incessantly stand on your head—
 Do you think, at your age, it is right?"

"In my youth," Father William replied to his son,
  "I feared it might injure the brain;
But, now that I'm perfectly sure I have none,
  Why, I do it again and again."

"You are old," said the youth, "as I mentioned before,
  And have grown most uncommonly fat;
Yet you turned a back-somersault in at the door—
  Pray, what is the reason of that?"

"In my youth," said the sage, as he shook his grey locks,
  "I kept all my limbs very supple
By the use of this ointment—one shilling the box—
  Allow me to sell you a couple?"

"You are old," said the youth, "and your jaws are too
      weak
  For anything tougher than suet;
Yet you finish the goose, with the bones and the beak—
  Pray, how do you manage to do it?"

"In my youth," said his father, "I took to the law,
  And argued each case with my wife;
And the muscular strength, which it gave to my jaw
  Has lasted the rest of my life."

"You are old," said the youth, "one would hardly suppose
  That your eye was as steady as ever;
Yet you balance an eel on the end of your nose—
  What made you so awfully clever?"

"I have answered three questions, and that is enough,"
  Said his father. "Don't give yourself airs!
Do you think I can listen all day to such stuff?
  Be off, or I'll kick you down-stairs!"

LEWIS CARROLL

97

There Is an Inn, a Merry Old Inn

There is an inn, a merry old inn
  beneath an old grey hill,
And there they brew a beer so brown
That the Man in the Moon himself came down
  one night to drink his fill.

The ostler has a tipsy cat
  that plays a five-stringed fiddle;
And up and down he runs his bow,
Now squeaking high, now purring low,
  now sawing in the middle.

The landlord keeps a little dog
  that is mighty fond of jokes;
When there's good cheer among the guests,
He cocks an ear at all the jests
  and laughs until he chokes.

They also keep a hornéd cow
  as proud as any queen;
But music turns her head like ale,
And makes her wave her tufted tail
  and dance upon the green.

And O! the rows of silver dishes
  and the store of silver spoons!
For Sunday there's a special pair,
And these they polish up with care
  on Saturday afternoons.

The Man in the Moon was drinking deep,
  and the cat began to wail;
A dish and a spoon on the table danced,
The cow in the garden madly pranced,
  and the little dog chased his tail.

The Man in the Moon took another mug,
  and then rolled beneath his chair;
And there he dozed and dreamed of ale,
Till in the sky the stars were pale,
  and dawn was in the air.

Then the ostler said to his tipsy cat:
  "The white horses of the Moon,
They neigh and champ their silver bits;
But their master's been and drowned his wits,
  and the Sun'll be rising soon!"

So the cat on his fiddle played hey-diddle-diddle,
  a jig that would wake the dead:
He squeaked and sawed and quickened the tune,
While the landlord shook the Man in the Moon:
  "It's after three!" he said.

They rolled the Man slowly up the hill
  and bundled him into the Moon,
While his horses galloped up in rear,
And the cow came capering like a deer,
  and a dish ran up with the spoon.

Now quicker the fiddle went deedle-dum-diddle;
　the dog began to roar,
The cow and the horses stood on their heads;
The guests all bounded from their beds
　and danced upon the floor.

With a ping and a pong the fiddle-strings broke!
　the cow jumped over the Moon,
And the little dog laughed to see such fun,
And the Saturday dish went off at a run
　With the silver Sunday spoon.

The round Moon rolled behind the hill,
　as the Sun raised up her head.
She* hardly believed her fiery eyes;
For though it was day, to her surprise
　they all went back to bed!

J. R. R. TOLKIEN

* Elves (and Hobbits) always refer to the Sun as She.

The Ship of Rio

There was a ship of Rio
    Sailed out into the blue,
And nine and ninety monkeys
    Were all her jovial crew.
From bo'sun to the cabin boy,
    From quarter to caboose,
There weren't a stitch of calico
    To breech 'em—tight or loose;
From spar to deck, from deck to keel,
    From barnacle to shroud,
There weren't one pair of reach-me-downs
    To all that jabbering crowd.
But wasn't it a gladsome sight,

When roared the deep-sea gales,
To see them reef her fore and aft,
  A-swinging by their tails!
Oh, wasn't it a gladsome sight,
  When glassy calm did come,
To see them squatting tailor-wise
  Around a keg of rum!
Oh, wasn't it a gladsome sight,
  When in she sailed to land,
To see them all a-scampering skip
  For nuts across the sand!

WALTER DE LA MARE

In Foreign Parts

When I lived in Singapore,
It was something of a bore
To receive the bulky Begums who came trundling to
    my door;
They kept getting into tangles
With their bingle-bongle-bangles,
And the tiger used to bite them as he sat upon the floor.

When I lived in Timbuctoo,
Almost every one I knew
Used to play upon the sackbut, singing "toodle-doodle-
    doo,"
And they made ecstatic ballads,
And consumed seductive salads,
Made of chicory and hickory and other things that grew.

When I lived in Rotterdam,
I possessed a spotted ram,
Who would never feed on anything but hollyhocks and
    ham;
But one day he butted down

All the magnates of the town,

So they slew him, though I knew him to be gentle as a
lamb.

But!

When I got to Kandahar,

It was very, very far,

And the people came and said to me, "How *very* plain
you are!"

So I sailed across the foam,

And I toddle-waddled home,

And no more I'll go a-rovering beyond the harbor bar.

LAURA E. RICHARDS

I'm Glad the Sky Is Painted Blue

I'm glad the sky is painted blue,
  And the earth is painted green,
With such a lot of nice fresh air
  All sandwiched in between.

Merry Are the Bells

Merry are the bells, and merry would they ring,
Merry was myself, and merry could I sing;
With a merry ding-dong, happy, gay, and free,
And a merry sing-song, happy let us be!

Waddle goes your gait, and hollow are your hose:
Noddle goes your pate, and purple is your nose:
Merry is your sing-song, happy, gay, and free;
With a merry ding-dong, happy let us be!

Merry have we met, and merry have we been;
Merry let us part, and merry meet again;
With our merry sing-song, happy, gay, and free,
With a merry ding-dong, happy let us be!

INDEX OF AUTHORS

INDEX OF TITLES

INDEX OF FIRST LINES